For Denys Cazet
—Daniel San Souci

Library of Congress Cataloging in Publication Data

San Souci, Daniel.
     The bedtime book.

     Summary: An illustrated collection of eleven folk and fairy
tales including "The Three Billy Goats Gruff," "Rapunzel," and
"The Sorcerer's Apprentice."
     1. Fairy tales.   [1. Fairy tales.   2. Folklore]
I. Title.
PZ8.S2477Be   1985   398.2'1   [E]   85-12898
ISBN 0-671-60505-4 (pbk.)
ISBN 0-671-60506-6 (lib. bdg.)

THE
BEDTIME BOOK

A Collection of Fairy Tales
Illustrated by Daniel San Souci

LITTLE SIMON
Published by Simon & Schuster, Inc., New York

10 9 8 7 6 5 4 3

The Three Billy Goats Gruff

**I**n a wide green valley, there once lived three billy goat brothers who were called Little Billy Goat Gruff, Middle-Sized Billy Goat Gruff, and Big Billy Goat Gruff. All day long the Billy Goats Gruff happily nibbled the grasses and flowers in the valley.

But one day they found that there were no more grasses and flowers to nibble. So they set out to climb the hillside to a new pasture.

Little Billy Goat Gruff had walked halfway up the hill when he came to a bridge across a stream. Now he didn't know it, but under the bridge lived a hideous Troll with sharp fangs, a straggly beard, and a nose as long as a poker.

Little Billy Goat Gruff stepped onto the bridge. *Trip, trap! Trip, trap!* went his feet.

"Who's that tripping over my bridge?" roared the Troll from below.

"It is I, Little Billy Goat Gruff."

"No one crosses my bridge!" shouted the Troll. "I am coming to gobble you up!"

"Oh, please, Troll, don't eat me," cried Little Billy Goat Gruff. "I'm much too little. Soon my brother will be along. He is fatter than I."

"Very well," said the Troll grumpily. "Be on your way then."

Presently, Middle-Sized Billy Goat Gruff reached the Troll's bridge. *Trip, trap! Trip, trap!* went his feet.

"Who's that tripping over my bridge?" roared the Troll.

"It is I, Middle-Sized Billy Goat Gruff."

"No one crosses my bridge! I am going to gobble you up!" yelled the Troll.

"Oh, no, please! Don't eat me. I'm too little.

Wait for my brother. He is much bigger than I."

"Very well," said the Troll. "Be off with you."

Soon Big Billy Goat Gruff reached the bridge. *TRIP, TRAP! TRIP, TRAP!* went his feet.

"Who's that tripping over my bridge?" roared the Troll.

"It is I, Big Billy Goat Gruff!"

"No one crosses my bridge! I am coming to gobble you up!"

"You do not frighten me," called Big Billy Goat Gruff. And he charged at the Troll, sending him hurtling into the stream. The Troll was never heard from again, but the Billy Goats Gruff are still in the pasture on the hill, growing fatter each day.

The Emperor's New Clothes

Many years ago there lived an Emperor who was so fond of new clothes that he spent all his money on them. He did not care about his soldiers; he did not care about going to the theater; he liked only to go out walking so he could show off his new clothes. He had an outfit for every hour in the day. In many cities an emperor's subjects often said, "The Emperor is in his council chambers," but in this city they said, "The Emperor is in his clothes closet."

In the Emperor's great city, life was always gay and exciting. Every day strangers came to visit. One day two strangers posing as weavers arrived. They said they knew how to make the most beautiful fabrics imaginable. Not only were the colors and patterns uncommonly fine, but the clothes cut from this cloth had the wonderful quality of being invisible to anyone who was stupid or dull or who was not fit for the office he held.

"Those must indeed be splendid clothes," thought the Emperor. "If I had them on I could find out which men in my kingdom are unfit for the offices they hold. I could tell those who are wise from the fools. This cloth must be woven for me at once." He gave the strangers a lot of money so that they could begin their work.

The impostors demanded the best gold thread with which to work, but they put it into their own bags. Then they sat down at two looms and pretended to weave—but there was not a thing on the shuttles. They worked at the empty looms till late into the night.

"I should like very much to know how far they have gotten with the cloth," thought the Emperor, but he decided not to look himself. What if he were unable to see the material? He wasn't really afraid that he was unfit to be Emperor, but he decided to send someone else to look the first time.

Everyone in town knew of the magical quality of the cloth and was eager to find out how silly or unwise his neighbors were.

"Well," thought the Emperor, "I will send my old and faithful minister to the weavers. He is a clever man, and surely he can judge what the cloth is like."

The good minister went into the hall where the two weavers sat working at the empty looms. "Dear me!" thought he, opening his eyes wide. "I can see nothing!" But he didn't say a word.

The two impostors begged him to be so kind as to step closer, and asked him if the cloth had not a beautiful texture and lovely colors. The poor minister bent toward the empty loom and rubbed his eyes, but still he saw nothing, for of course, there was nothing to see.

"Good heavens!" thought he. "Can I be stupid and unfit for my office? I do not see a thing on the loom."

"Tell us, my good man. What do you think of our work?" asked one of the weavers.

"Oh, it is lovely, most lovely," answered the old minister, peering through his glasses. "What a texture! What colors! Yes, I will tell the Emperor that it pleases me very much."

"And that pleases *us*," said the impostors. Then they told the minister just what colors they were using and what patterns they were weaving. The minister listened very carefully so that he could repeat their words to the Emperor.

After the minister had made his report, the impostors wanted more money and more gold thread for their looms, which they promptly put into their own pockets. The shuttles remained empty.

In a few weeks, the Emperor sent another trusted statesman to see how the fabulous cloth was coming along.

His Majesty

The statesman looked and looked but, like the minister, he could not see a thing.

Now, the statesman knew he was not stupid, so he said to himself, "It must be that I am not fit for my office, but no one must be allowed to know it. This is very odd, however." And so he praised the cloth, which he did not see, and the told the impostors he was delighted with the beautiful colors and splendid texture.

"Yes, it is quite handsome," he reported back to the Emperor. "It is the most lovely piece of cloth I have ever seen."

By now, everyone in town was talking of the magnificent cloth, and the Emperor decided that he wanted to see it himself while it was still on the looms. With a great crowd of followers, among them the two worthy statesmen who had already made their glowing reports, he went to the impostors. They were weaving with all their might, but without fiber or thread.

"Is it not splendid?" cried both the old statesmen. "See, Your Majesty! What a texture! What colors!" And then they pointed to the empty looms, for they believed that the others could see

the cloth quite well.

"What is this?" thought the Emperor. "I can see nothing! This is indeed horrible. Am I stupid? Am I not fit to be Emperor? That would certainly be dreadful." But he said to the two weavers, "It is indeed the most beautiful cloth. It has my most gracious approval." Then he nodded pleasantly and examined the empty looms, for he could think of nothing further to say.

His whole court looked and looked and saw no more than the others, but they, like the Emperor, said, "Oh! It is beautiful!" And they advised him to wear these magnificent new clothes for the first time at a procession that was soon to take place during a great celebration.

Throughout the night, the two weavers busily prepared the Emperor's new clothes for the procession. They pretended they were taking the cloth from the loom, cutting it with huge scissors in the air, and sewing it with threadless needles. At last they said, "Now the Emperor's new clothes are finished!"

The Emperor went to the weavers with his distinguished knights, and each impostor raised his arm as if he were holding something up, and he said, "See! Here are the breeches! Here is the coat! Here is the cloak! And this," they announced grandly, "is the most splendid train we have ever made.

"The cloth is so delicate and comfortable that one might imagine one has nothing on at all; but that is the beauty of it! Will Your Majesty graciously take off his clothes?" said the impostors. "Then we will put on the new clothes, here in front of the mirror."

The Emperor took off all his clothes, and the impostors stood before him and pretended to put on each new article of clothing. They pretended to button buttons and tie sashes and fasten buckles.

"How beautifully the clothes fit! How they suit you!" exclaimed everybody. "What a texture! What colors! They are gorgeous robes!"

The Master of Ceremonies for the festivities announced, "They are waiting outside with the canopy that is to be carried over you."

"I am ready," said the Emperor. And he turned again to the mirror to see if his finery was on all right.

Two chamberlains were to carry the Emperor's train as he stepped out to the canopy. They put their hands near the floor as if they were picking it up; then they lifted their hands high in the air as if they were holding something. They did not want anyone to think that they could see nothing.

So the Emperor went along in the procession, and all the people in the streets and at the windows said, "How perfect are the Emperor's new clothes!" No one wished his neighbors to believe that he could see nothing, for then he would have been unfit for his office, or else very stupid.

"But he has nothing on!" exclaimed a little child at last.

"Just listen to the innocent child," said the father, and each person whispered to his neighbor what the child had said.

The Emperor thought that the child was right, but he told himself, "I must go on with the procession now. I can't turn back." And so the Emperor walked on more proudly than ever, and the chamberlains stooped to pick up his train—which was not there at all.

Red Riding Hood

 nce there was a sweet little girl who was loved by all who knew her. But she was most loved by her grandmother, who sewed her a red velvet hood. It looked so becoming on the girl that she never wore anything else over her dress, and thereafter everyone called her Red Riding Hood.

One day, Red Riding Hood's mother said to her, "Take these cakes and this pot of butter to your grandmother. She is weak and ill, and they will do her good. And promise me you will not talk to strangers on the way."

Red Riding Hood promised; then she set out carrying the cakes and butter in a basket on her arm. Her grandmother lived on the other side of a forest, so Red Riding Hood had a long walk before her. As soon as she came to the woods, she met a wolf.

"Good day, Red Riding Hood," said the wolf sweetly, with a bow.

"Good morning," replied Red Riding Hood, forgetting the promise she had made her mother.

"Where are you going so early, my child?" asked the wolf.

"To my grandmother's. She is ill, and I am bringing some food to her."

"And where does your grandmother live?"

"At the end of the forest path," replied Red Riding Hood. "Her house is the first one past the woods."

The wolf thought to himself, "This tender little girl would be even more delicious than her grandmother. I must manage somehow to catch both of them."

"Good day," he said to Red Riding Hood and ran to the grandmother's house as fast as his legs would carry him. But Red Riding Hood walked slowly, stopping to pick a bouquet of flowers for her grandmother.

When the wolf reached the grandmother's house, he knocked at the door—*tap, tap.*

"Who's there?" called Grandmother.

"It is Red Riding Hood," said the wolf in a high voice.

"Lift the latch, my dearest," said Grandmother. "I am too feeble to get up."

So the wolf sprang into the grandmother's house and gobbled her up. Then he put on her clothes and her cap, and got into her bed.

Soon Red Riding Hood came knocking at the door—*tap, tap.*

"Who's there?" called the wolf.

Red Riding Hood thought Grandmother's voice sounded odd, but she decided that Grandmother had a bad cold and was hoarse. So she answered, "It is Red Riding Hood, bringing you a basket of food."

"Lift the latch, my sweet," replied the wolf. "I am too feeble to get up."

Red Riding Hood entered the cottage and stood by Grandmother's bed. "Why, Grandmother!" she exclaimed. "What big ears you have."

"The better to hear you with, my dear," answered the wolf.

"And Grandmother, what big eyes you have."

"The better to see you with, my dear."

"And Grandmother, what big hands you have."

"The better to hold you with, my dear," replied the wolf.

"And Grandmother," Red Riding Hood said, feeling frightened, "What big teeth you have."

"The better to eat you with, my dear!" cried the wolf. And he leapt out of the bed and ate up Red Riding Hood in one big gulp.

Then the wolf, full from his meal, crawled back into the bed to take a nap. Soon he was snoring loudly. A huntsman heard him as he passed by, and he thought, "How the old woman snores! I had better see if there is anything wrong with her."

When the huntsman saw the wolf lying asleep in the bed, he cried, "At last I find you, you old sinner!" He was about to shoot the wolf when he decided that the wolf might have swallowed the grandmother whole, and that she still might be saved. So instead, he took a pair of shears and began to slit open the wolf's belly. When he had made a few snips, out popped Red Riding Hood, followed shortly by Grandmother. Both were most grateful to the huntsman.

Red Riding Hood quickly fetched some large stones, and filled the wolf's belly with them. Later he awoke and was about to rush away, but the stones were so heavy that he sank down dead.

Red Riding Hood, Grandmother, and the huntsman were very pleased. The huntsman took off the Wolf's skin and carried it home; the grandmother ate the cakes with the butter; and Red Riding Hood said to herself that from now on she would not talk to strangers and would mind what her mother told her.

The Story of the Three Bears

nce upon a time there were three bears who lived in a house in the woods. The baby bear was a little, small, wee bear; the mother was a middle-sized bear; and the father bear was a great, huge bear. Each had a pot for porridge—a little one for the little, small, wee bear; a middle-sized one for the middle bear; and a great one for the great, huge bear. Each had a chair to sit in—a little chair for the little, small, wee bear; a middle-sized chair for the middle bear; and a great chair for the great, huge bear. And each had a bed to sleep in—a little bed for the little, small, wee bear; a middle-

sized bed for the middle bear; and a great bed for the great, huge bear.

One day, after they had made the porridge for their breakfast and poured it into their porridge pots, they took a walk in the woods while the porridge was cooling. While they were walking, a little old woman came to their house. She was not a good honest old woman, for, seeing nobody in the house, she lifted the latch, opened the door, and went in. And she was very pleased when she saw the porridge on the table. If she had been a good little old woman she would have waited till the bears came home, and then perhaps they would have asked her to breakfast. But she was an impudent, bad old woman, and she set about helping herself.

First she tasted the porridge of the great, huge bear. That was too hot for her. Then she tasted the porridge of the middle bear. That was too cold for her. And then she went to the porridge of the little, small, wee bear, and tasted that. It was neither too hot nor too cold, but just right, and she liked it so well that she ate it all up.

Then the little old woman sat down in the chair of the great, huge bear, but that was too hard for her. She sat down in the chair of the middle bear, but that was too soft for her. And then she sat down in the chair of the little, small, wee bear, and that was neither too hard nor too soft, but just right. So she sat in it till the bottom of the chair came out, and down she came, plump upon the ground.

Then the little old woman went upstairs into the bedchamber in which the three bears slept. First she lay down on the bed of the great, huge bear; but that was too high at the head for her. Next she lay down upon the bed of the middle bear; that was too high at the foot for her. Then she lay down upon the bed of the little, small, wee bear; and that was just right. So she covered herself up comfortably and lay there till she fell asleep.

By this time the three bears thought their porridge would be cool enough, so they came home to breakfast.

"SOMEBODY HAS BEEN AT MY POR-RIDGE!" said the great, huge bear in his great, gruff voice, when he saw his porridge pot.

SOMEBODY HAS BEEN AT MY POR-RIDGE!" said the middle bear in her middle voice, when she saw her porridge pot.

Then the little, small, wee bear looked at his porridge pot. "Somebody has been at my porridge, and has eaten it all up!" he said in his little, small, wee voice.

Now the three bears saw that someone had entered their house and they began to look about.

"SOMEBODY HAS BEEN SITTING IN MY CHAIR!" said the great, huge bear in his great, rough, gruff voice.

"SOMEBODY HAS BEEN SITTING IN MY CHAIR!" said the middle bear in her middle voice.

"Somebody has been sitting in my chair, and has pushed the bottom out of it!" said the little, small, wee bear in his little, small, wee voice.

Then the three bears went upstairs into their bed chamber.

"SOMEBODY HAS BEEN LYING IN MY BED!" said the great, huge bear in his great, rough, gruff voice.

"SOMEBODY HAS BEEN LYING IN MY

BED!" said the middle bear in her middle voice.

And when the little, small, wee bear came to look at his bed, there was the little old woman.

"Somebody has been lying in my bed—and here she is!" said the little, small, wee bear in his little, small, wee voice.

The little old woman had heard in her sleep the great, rough, gruff voice of the great, huge bear, but she was so fast asleep that it was no more to her than the roaring of wind or the rumbling of thunder.

And she had heard the middle voice of the middle bear, but it was only as if she had heard someone speaking in a dream.

But when she heard the little, small, wee voice of the little, small, wee bear, it was so sharp and so shrill that it awakened her at once.

She sat right up, and when she saw the three bears on one side of the bed, she tumbled out the other and ran to the window as fast as she could. The window was open and out it the little old woman jumped. The bad little old woman disappeared into the woods, and the three bears never saw anything more of her.

Rapunzel

 here once lived a man and his wife who had wished for a child for a long time, and at last it seemed that their wish was to come true, for the wife was going to have a baby.

Now at the back of their house was a little window which overlooked a beautiful garden full of lovely flowers and shrubs. It was, however, surrounded by a wall, and nobody dared to enter because it belonged to a witch who was greatly feared.

One day the woman stood at the window looking into the garden and saw a bed planted with rampion. It looked so fresh and green that she longed to eat some of it. Day after day she looked at it. The more she looked at it, the more she wanted to eat it, but she knew she would never be able to, so she began to grow pale and miserable. When

her husband became alarmed and asked, "What is the matter, dear wife?" she answered, "Alas, if I cannot get any of the rampion to eat from the garden behind our house, I shall die."

The man loved his wife very much, and he thought to himself, "I cannot lose her. I will get the rampion no matter what the risk."

So at twilight he climbed over the wall into the witch's garden, hastily picked a handful of rampion, and took it back to his wife. She immediately prepared it and ate it eagerly. It was so very, very good that the next day she wanted it three times as badly as before. Her husband realized that if he were to get any rest, he would have to go back to the garden. So at twilight her husband set out again, but when he got over the wall the witch was waiting for him.

"How dare you come into my garden like a

thief and steal my rampion?" she cried angrily.

"Alas!" he answered. "I am only here because my wife has such a longing for it that she says she will die if she cannot get some."

Then the witch said to him, "I will allow you to take away with you as much rampion as you like, on the condition that you give me the child your wife is about to bring into this world. I shall care for it like a mother."

The man was so frightened that he agreed to everything. And when the baby was born, the witch came to take her away. She named her Rapunzel, which means rampion.

Rapunzel was the most beautiful child under the sun. When she was twelve, the witch shut her up in a tower in the midst of the woods. The tower had no staircase and no door, only a window high up in the wall.

Rapunzel had splendid long hair as fine as spun gold. When the witch wanted to enter the tower she cried, "Rapunzel, Rapunzel, let down your hair!" As soon as Rapunzel heard the witch, she unfastened her long braid and let it fall to the ground below, and the witch would climb up it.

It happened that a few years later the King's son rode through the forest near the tower. He heard a song so lovely he stopped to listen. It was Rapunzel, who in her loneliness sang sweet songs to pass away the time. The King's son wanted to join her, and he looked for the door, but there was none. So he rode home. But he could not forget about Rapunzel, and every day he returned to the forest to listen to her sing. Then one day, as he was standing under a tree, he saw the witch arrive and heard her call, "Rapunzel, Rapunzel, let down your hair!" He watched as the witch climbed into the tower, remained there for some time, and then climbed down.

"So," the Prince thought, "since that is the ladder, I will climb it and seek my fortune."

He went away again, but the next evening he returned to the forest, waited for dusk, and called out as the witch had done previously, "Rapunzel, Rapunzel, let down your hair!"

The hair fell down and the King's son climbed up it.

At first Rapunzel was terrified, for she had never seen a man before. But when he talked to her kindly and told her how deeply moved he had been by her song, Rapunzel lost her fear. And when he asked her to marry him, she thought, "Why not? I will certainly like him better than my old mother."

So she held her hand out to the Prince and said, "Yes, but you must help me get down from this tower. Each time you come to visit me, bring me a skein of silk and I will twist it into a ladder and climb down. Then you can take me away from here." They agreed that the King's son should visit Rapunzel every evening, since the old woman only came during the day.

Their secret would have been safe if Rapunzel had not made one mistake. One day she was waiting for the witch to climb her hair, and she forgot and said, "How is it that you climb so slowly when the King's son can be up here in a moment?"

At that, the witch was furious. "You wicked girl!" she cried. "I thought I had hidden you from all the world, but I see you have betrayed me!" In her rage, she seized Rapunzel's beautiful hair,

snatched up a pair of shears, and cut off the braid. She took Rapunzel away into the wilderness, where she forced her to live in grief and misery.

That evening the witch returned to the tower and fastened Rapunzel's long braid to the window. When the Prince came he called, "Rapunzel, Rapunzel, let down your hair," and the witch lowered the hair. The Prince climbed up, but there, instead of his beloved Rapunzel, he found the witch.

"You've come to fetch your ladylove, have you?" the witch cackled. "Well, she's gone. She's lost to you and you'll never set eyes on her again."

The Prince was so filled with grief that he leapt from the tower window. He escaped with his life, but he fell into a bramble bush, which put out both of his eyes. After that, he wandered about completely blind in the woods, living on roots and berries, weeping and lamenting the loss of his beloved wife.

In this way he wandered for some years until one day he came to the place in the wilderness where the witch had left Rapunzel. She lived there now with her twin children, for she had borne the Prince a son and a daughter. The Prince heard a voice that sounded familiar, and he went toward it. Rapunzel knew him at once and fell to weeping upon his neck. Two of her tears fell upon his eyes, which suddenly grew quite clear, and he could see as well as ever.

The Prince took Rapunzel to his kingdom, where his father met them both with great joy, and there they lived in happiness for the rest of their lives.

Snow White

any winters ago, a Queen gave birth to a lovely child with skin as white as the snow outside the window. But the Queen died shortly thereafter, whispering the name she had chosen for her little daughter—Snow White.

A year later, the King took another wife who was beautiful but very proud. Each day she would stand before her magic looking glass and say:

Mirror, mirror on the wall,
Who's the fairest of them all?

And the mirror, which could not lie, would answer:

You are the fairest one of all.

However, little Snow White was growing more and more beautiful, and one day when the Queen asked the mirror her question, it replied:

Queen, you are full fair, 'tis true,
But young Snow White is fairer than you.

The Queen was shocked to hear this, and before long she could think of nothing but to be rid of the girl forever. So she called for her huntsman and said, "Take Snow White into the woods and put her to death."

The huntsman agreed and led Snow White away. But he was unable to kill her. Instead he said, "Away with you. Go into the wild woods, and never return."

When poor Snow White found herself alone in the woods, she was very frightened and ran through the trees until she arrived at a shingled cottage standing in a small clearing. She entered the cottage, lay down upon a bed, and fell asleep.

That evening the masters of the house came home. They were seven dwarfs who spent their days mining the mountains. When they found Snow White lying on the bed, they were filled with joy at the sight of her, and they let her sleep on.

In the morning, Snow White awoke and quickly became friends with the seven kindly dwarfs. She offered to keep house for them, and in return they promised to care for her always. So Snow White stayed at the cottage.

Now the Queen, supposing that Snow White was dead, stood before the magic looking glass again and asked her question, and the mirror replied:

> Queen, thou art of beauty rare,
> But Snow White living in a glen,
> With the seven little men,
> Is a thousand times more fair.

The Queen became angry at this, and she plotted to put an end to the girl once and for all. She disguised herself as an old peddler and visited the dwarfs' cottage. "Come taste this apple, my pretty," she said when Snow White answered the door. "Tell me if you'd like some to bake in a pie for supper tonight."

Snow White had not yet begun her baking for the day, and so she tasted the fruit. But the instant she took a bite, she fell down as though dead.

"Now you are no longer the fairest," said the old woman as she hurried away.

Toward evening the seven dwarfs returned home. They were terrified to see Snow White lying on the ground. They picked her up and tried everything they could think of to revive her, but nothing worked. At last they placed her on a bier and wept for three days.

After the three days had passed, the dwarfs built Snow White a casket of glass. They set it out upon the mountain they were mining, so that they might watch over her as they worked.

One day a Prince rode through the woods and, spying the casket, looked upon Snow White and fell deeply in love with her. "Please let me take the casket with me to my castle so that I might look upon lovely Snow White every day," the Prince said to the dwarfs.

The dwarfs took pity on the Prince and consented, and the King's son bid his servants to carry the casket away on their shoulders.

But it happened that as the servants were going along bearing their burden, one stumbled over a bush. The jolt dislodged the bit of poison apple from Snow White's throat and set it flying from her mouth.

"Oh, dear!" cried Snow White, wide awake. "Where am I?"

"You are with me, beloved," answered the Prince, full of joy. "Come to my father's castle and be my bride."

Snow White went with the Prince, and their wedding was held in great splendor. But being a good and gentle girl, Snow White never forgot the kindness of the dwarfs, for every fortnight she held a banquet especially for them in the Palace Hall.

The Elves and the Shoemaker

There was once a shoemaker who had become so poor that he had nothing left but enough leather to make just one pair of shoes. That evening, after a meager meal of soup and bread, he cut out the shoes, set the pieces out on the workbench to be stitched the next day, and sadly went to bed.

When he awoke the next morning, he was greeted by an amazing sight: sitting on his workbench was a finished pair of shoes, sewn with stitches so small he needed his spectacles to see them.

"It would take me days to stitch a shoe so fine. What magic is this?" exclaimed the shoemaker to his wife.

"Surely it is good magic," she answered.

Soon after, a customer entered the shop and was so pleased with the shoes that he bought them on the spot and paid a very high price for them.

The shoemaker now had enough money to buy the leather for two pairs of shoes. He cut the pieces out that evening, and, once again, set them on his workbench for the morning. But when he arose, they were already finished. And right away, two customers came into the shop and offered to pay so much for the new shoes that the shoemaker was able to buy leather enough for four more pairs.

Early the next morning he found the four pairs also finished, and so it happened that whatever he cut out in the evening was stitched into the finest shoes imaginable by morning. Before long, the shoemaker was making a handsome living and had grown quite rich.

One night, not long before Christmas, when the shoemaker had finished cutting out the pieces of leather to be stitched into shoes, he turned to his wife and said, "Let us sit up tonight and see who is making us so wealthy."

His wife agreed, and they hid in a corner of the room behind a curtain and waited. As soon as the clock struck midnight, two little elves entered the workshop through the window. At once, they seated themselves before the shoemaker's table and began to stitch and hammer the leather into shoes with such nimble little fingers that the shoemaker could scarcely believe his eyes. When they had finished, they scampered out the window, leaving behind a workbench neatly lined with dozens of pairs of shoes.

The next morning, the shoemaker's wife said, "Those little men have helped us put meat on the table. Now we should do something for them. I can make them two new, warm outfits, and you can stitch each a pair of shoes."

The shoemaker agreed, and the couple set to work at once. After they had finished, they laid the gifts together on the table in place of the leather the shoemaker usually left on the workbench. Then they hid themselves behind the curtain and waited for the little men's arrival.

When midnight came, the elves scampered in, ready to begin work, but discovered, much to their delight, the tiny suits of clothes and even tinier pairs of shoes. With a giggle and a laugh, they put on their new outfits, danced an elfin jig round the workbench, and skippity-hopped right out the window.

The two little men never returned after that night, but they left good fortune behind, for the shoemaker and his wife were never poor again.

The Twelve Dancing Princesses

nce upon a time there lived a young shepherd boy. His name was Michael, but everyone called him Star Gazer because he was such a dreamer.

One hot summer's morning, while Michael was supposed to be tending the sheep, he fell asleep under a tree. He dreamed that a beautiful lady dressed in a robe of gold appeared before him and said, "Go to the castle of Beloeil, and there you shall marry a Princess."

Now one of Michael's wishes had always been that he would fall in love with a Princess and marry her. So Michael believed the golden-robed lady, and he decided to go immediately to Beloeil. Although the villagers laughed at him, Michael made his clothes into a bundle and said good-bye to all his friends.

It was known the land over that in the castle of Beloeil there lived twelve Princesses of wonderful beauty. All slept together in one room, their twelve beds in a long row. Each day they slept far into the morning, and it was whispered that, although the King locked and bolted their door each night, the next day their satin shoes were found worn into holes, as if the Princesses had danced all night.

When asked what they had been doing all night, the Princesses would never admit that they had been doing anything but sleeping. However, the King did not believe them, and he was determined to discover the truth.

It so happened that, not long before Michael came to the castle, the King issued a proclamation. It said that whoever could discover how his daughters wore out their shoes each night could choose one of them for his wife. Very shortly a Prince arrived at the palace, saying he wished to try his luck at discovering the Princesses' secret. He was given a room next door to the Princesses' bedchamber. He planned to stay up all night, keeping watch to see when the Princesses left their room, to find out where they danced. But the Prince quickly grew heavy-eyed and soon fell asleep. The next morning, twelve pairs of satin slippers were danced to pieces, as usual—and the Prince was nowhere to be seen.

After this a number of Princes waited up all night watching the Princesses' door, but when morning came each Prince in turn disappeared. No one could tell what had become of him or what the Princesses had done to wear out their slippers.

By the time Michael arrived at Beloeil, quite a few Princes had tried to discover the secret but had disappeared instead. Michael went to work for the castle gardener. His job was to bring each Princess a bouquet every morning. The Princesses took the bouquets from him without deigning to look at him—except Lina, the youngest, who gazed at him with her large black eyes the first morning and exclaimed, "Oh, how pretty he is—our new flower boy!" And the other Princesses burst out laughing.

That night the Star Gazer had a dream. The lady in the golden dress appeared before him for a second time. This time she was holding in one hand two young laurel trees, and in the other hand she held a little golden rake, a little golden bucket, and a silken towel.

She said, "Plant these laurels in two large pots, smooth them over with the rake, water them from the bucket, and wipe them with the towel.

When they have grown as tall as a girl of fifteen, they will grant you whatever you wish."

When Michael awoke, he found the two laurel bushes beside him. So he carefully obeyed the orders. The trees grew very fast, and when they were tall enough, he asked them to make him invisible. Then there appeared on the laurel a pretty white flower, which Michael put into his buttonhole.

That evening, when the Princesses went upstairs to bed, Michael followed them barefoot, so that he might make no noise, and hid himself under one of their beds. When he peeped out, he saw that the twelve sisters had donned splendid garments and wore satin shoes on their feet. In their hands they carried the bouquets he had brought them.

"Are you ready?" asked the eldest Princess.

"Yes," replied the other eleven in chorus. And the eldest Princess crossed the room to her bed and tapped it. The bed sank through the floor and a secret stairway was revealed. It led a long way down, and as the eldest Princess stepped along it, she disappeared into darkness. The other Prin-

cesses followed her, with the invisible Michael close at their heels.

After a time they passed through a door and found themselves in some lovely woods where the leaves were spangled with drops of pure silver. They walked through the woods and came to other woods where the leaves were sprinkled with pure gold. And after that they came to yet other woods where the leaves glittered with real diamonds. At last Michael found himself by a large lake. Along the shore were twelve little boats in which were seated twelve Princes, each awaiting his Princess.

Each Princess climbed daintily into a boat with her Prince, and Michael slipped into the boat with the youngest Princess. The Princes began rowing and, before long, the boats reached the far side of the lake. There Michael saw a brightly lit castle. From outside he could hear music—trumpets blaring and drums beating. The Princes helped the Princesses ashore, and Michael tiptoed behind them as they entered the castle.

Inside was a magnificent ballroom. Michael stood in a corner to watch the dancers. Never had he seen so many beautiful Princesses together at

one time. But the one whom he thought the most beautiful was Lina. The Princesses danced and danced until their slippers were worn into holes. When morning came and the cock crowed, a meal was served. At the meal the Princes were made to drink drafts from golden cups, which froze their hearts and left nothing in them but the love of dancing.

On the way back, passing through the woods, Michael broke off one of the silver branches. The next day, as he made up the Princesses' bouquets, he hid the branch with the silver drops in the bouquet intended for the youngest Princess.

When Lina discovered it, she was surprised but said nothing to her sisters. Once during the day, she met Michael by accident and started to speak to him, but she decided against it and went on her way.

That night the Star Gazer again followed the Princesses to the ballroom and again watched them dance. And as they were returning that morning Michael broke off a gold-spangled branch as they passed through the forest of golden trees. The next day, when Lina found the branch in her bouquet, she went to Michael. This time, feeling frightened, she demanded to know how he had come upon it.

"Your Royal Highness knows well enough," answered Michael.

"You know our secret! Please, you must keep it!" cried Lina, and she flung a purse of shining gold at the boy.

"I will not sell my silence," said the boy, and he went away without picking up the purse.

Lina's sisters had seen her talking with the gardener boy and made fun of her.

"Why don't you marry him?" they teased. "You could become a gardener too and bring us our bouquets."

The little Princess was so angry that she

wanted to scare her sisters as she had been scared. She told them Michael knew of their secret. They met and decided among themselves to invite Michael that night to come dancing with them and, when the time came, to give him the draft that would enchant him as it had frozen the hearts of the Princes.

So the Princesses invited him and Michael consented to go, even though he knew the fate they had planned for him. He had already decided to sacrifice himself so that he could forever dance with his beloved Lina. Once again he called upon the laurel to grant him a wish, this time that he be dressed like a prince.

The laurel worked its magic. A beautiful pink flower appeared and Michael found himself clothed in velvet as black as the eyes of the little Princess.

That night in the great ballroom, Michael and the little Princess danced every dance together. At dawn, when he was leading her to her seat at the meal table, she said, "Here you are—all your wishes are coming true. You are being treated like a prince."

"Don't be afraid," replied the Star Gazer, "you shall never be a gardener's wife, but always a prince's princess."

The little Princess did not answer him but stared at him with a frightened face.

It soon came time for the draft to be served to Michael. He raised the golden cup, cast a lingering glance at the little Princess, and prepared to swallow.

"Don't drink!" cried out the little Princess. "I would rather marry a gardener." And she burst into tears.

Michael flung the cup behind him and fell at Lina's feet. The rest of the Princes fell at the feet of the other Princesses. The charm was broken.

That morning Michael and the Princesses crossed the lake and passed through the three woods. They went to the King. Michael held out the golden cup and revealed the secret of the holes in the shoes.

"Choose, then," said the King. "You may have whomever of my daughters you prefer."

"My choice has already been made," replied the Star Gazer, and he offered his hand to Lina, who blushed and lowered her eyes.

So the Princess did not become a gardener's wife; on the contrary, the Star Gazer became a Prince. But before the marriage ceremony, the Princess insisted that Michael tell her how he came to discover the secret.

Michael showed her the two laurels that had helped him, and she, being prudent and thinking they would give him too much advantage over his wife, cut them off at the root and threw them into the fire.

When the wedding took place, it was a grand celebration indeed. The eleven sisters of the youngest Princess served as the bridesmaids, and after the ceremony the guests and the Princesses danced till dawn. The Princesses wore out all their slippers again, but this time no one minded.

Afterwards Michael and Lina lived happily for the rest of their days. And they always did like to dance.

The Three Little Pigs

Once upon a time there was a mother pig who sent her three little pigs out into the world to seek their fortunes.

The first little pig met a man carrying a bundle of straw.

"Please, sir," said the little pig, "will you sell me some of your straw to build a house?"

The man sold him the straw, and the first little pig had just put the finishing touches on his house when there came a knock on the door.

A big bad wolf said, "Little Pig, Little Pig, let me come in!"

"No, not by the hair on my chinny chin chin," replied the first little pig.

"Then I'll huff, and I'll puff, and I'll blow your house in!" cried the big bad wolf.

So the wolf huffed, and he puffed, and he blew the house down. And he ate up that fat little pig.

The second little pig met a man carrying a load of sticks.

"Please, sir," said the little pig, "will you sell me some of your sticks to build a house?"

The man sold him the sticks, and the second little pig had just put the finishing touches on his house when the big bad wolf came knocking on his door.

"Little Pig, Little Pig, let me come in!"

"No, not by the hair on my chinny chin chin."

"Then I'll huff, and I'll puff, and I'll blow your house in!"

So the big bad wolf huffed, and he puffed, and he puffed, and he huffed, and he blew that house down. Then he ate up the second little pig.

The third little pig met a man carrying a load of bricks.

"Please, sir," said the little pig, "will you sell me some of your bricks to build a house?"

The man sold him the bricks, and the little pig built his house, but it took much longer than building a house of straw or sticks. He was just putting the last brick into place when the big bad wolf knocked at the door.

"Little Pig, Little Pig, let me come in!"

"No, not by the hair on my chinny chin chin!"

"Then I'll huff, and I'll puff, and I'll blow your house in!"

So the big bad wolf huffed, and he puffed, and he puffed, and he huffed, and he huffed, and he puffed some more, but try as he might, he could not blow that house down.

But the big bad wolf would not give up. "Little Pig, Little Pig!" he called. "I know where you can get some nice plump turnips."

"Where?" asked the third little pig.

"In the field down the road. If you like, we can go to the field together tomorrow morning. We can get some turnips for supper."

"All right," said the little pig, who liked turnips very much. But the next morning he woke up early and got the turnips before the wolf arrived.

When the wolf found out, he was angry, but still he would not give up. "I know where you can

get some juicy red apples," he said.

"Where?" asked the third little pig.

"In the garden down the road. If you like, we can go to the garden early tomorrow morning, and I will show you where the juiciest apples are."

"Very well," replied the third little pig. He liked apples almost as much as he liked turnips. But the next morning he woke up even earlier, went to the garden, and found the apples himself. He was high up in a tree, just about to start on his way home, when he spied the big bad wolf coming toward him. The little pig was frightened indeed.

"Ha! Little Pig," exclaimed the wolf. "So you have found the apples."

"Yes," replied the third little pig. "Wait. I will toss one to you."

And he did, but he threw it so far that the wolf could not find it. While the wolf was looking for it, the third little pig ran all the way home to his house of bricks.

When the big bad wolf realized he had been tricked again, he became angrier than ever before. He decided to eat up the third little pig then and there.

"Little Pig, Little Pig," he called, "I'm coming in. You can't save yourself, for I'll come down the chimney!"

"Come right ahead," replied the third pig, for he had put a pot of water on the fire in his hearth, and it was boiling away.

So the big bad wolf, feeling very clever, came down the chimney and landed right in the boiling water.

And that was the end of the big bad wolf.

The Sorcerer's Apprentice

 man one day found himself needing a helper for his work-shop, so he decided to search for an apprentice. On the very first day of his search, he had not walked far from the cottage in which he lived, when he met a boy walking through the woods.

Now it so happened that the lad was just setting out to make his fortune in the world, so he was quite pleased when the man said to him, "I need an apprentice. Can you read and write?"

"Indeed I can, sir!" said the eager lad.

"What a shame," said the man. "I can't use you then. I am looking for someone who can neither read nor write."

"Excuse me, sir," said the quick-witted lad. "I guess I misunderstood you. *Read* and *write*, did you say? I'm afraid I can't read or write at all. Not one single word."

"Very good, then," said the man. "Come to my workshop and I'll put you to work."

Now, the lad knew perfectly well how to read and write, and it seemed strange to him that a man should want a worker who could do neither. So the new apprentice decided to do his job but to keep his eyes and ears open.

The man led the boy into the little workshop by his cottage. As soon as the boy entered, he saw that it was a dark and gruesome place. Cobwebs hung from every beam. The shelves sagged with great, dusty books, glass beakers, and jars containing mysterious powders and steaming liquids. Over the fire, a giant cauldron boiled and bubbled.

"So," the lad thought to himself, "this new employer of mine must be a sorcerer or a magician! What a lot I can learn from him! With some chants and some charms I can never go wrong. I might even be able to do some good in the world." And the lad pretended to be very stupid, but all along he was paying close attention to the sorcerer.

The lad did everything he was told. Every day he stirred the foul brew that simmered in the cauldron. Every afternoon he ground herbs in the enormous mortar, using an enormous pestle. Every evening he fetched wood to start the next morning's fire.

As the days went by, the apprentice became more and more curious. Just what was the sorcerer up to? More than anything, the boy longed to look at the thick, dusty books on the sorcerer's shelf. He knew they contained all sorts of delicious mysterious spells. But since he was not supposed to know how to read, the boy didn't dare open them.

One night, however, he could wait no longer. "Surely," he thought, "I can safely take just one peek at one book while my master sleeps." So when the lad was certain the sorcerer was asleep, he crept from bed and carefully took down one of the large books. The pages were a mass of mystic symbols, formulas for spells, and recipes for potions. The apprentice was fascinated, and he found that he could not stop reading. He pored over the ancient pages until dawn, when he crept back to bed again, his head swimming with magic.

Every night thereafter the lad waited until his employer was asleep, then he studied the books in the sorcerer's library. The more he read, the more convinced he became that his employer was a *wicked* sorcerer.

The boy then thought up a daring plan. Whenever the sorcerer was out during the day, the apprentice practiced casting spells. He turned the cat into a canary and then back into a cat again. He turned the broom into a rosebush and then back into a broom again.

But one day the sorcerer returned early and caught the lad in the middle of casting a spell.

"Liar!" he cried. "You *can* read and write. And you've stolen my secrets."

He rushed to the lad, hoping to toss him into the boiling cauldron, but the apprentice was too swift for him.

The boy muttered one of the spells he had learned and—*whoosh!*—turned himself into a bird! But the sorcerer was not to be outdone. He thought quickly and—*whoosh!*—turned himself into a larger bird and chased the boy as he flew through the woods, pecking at his head.

Then the lad changed himself into a fish and jumped into a pond. The sorcerer turned into a bigger fish and dived after him. The boy turned himself into an even bigger fish and turned on the sorcerer. To save himself, the sorcerer summoned all his powers, changed himself into a kernel of corn, and lodged himself between two stones beside the pond—beyond the lad's reach. Quick as a wink, the boy turned himself into a rooster. With his beak, he dug out the kernel and ate it, thus bringing an end to the evil sorcerer.

And so it was that the apprentice became a sorcerer. From that day to this, he has used his powers to perform good magic only.

The Bremen Town Musicians

 n old donkey, who realized that his master had begun to think of turning him out, once decided to travel to Bremen to find a job as a town musician. When he had gone just a little way, he met a dog lying by the side of the road, panting as if he had run a long way.

"What are you so out of breath about?" asked the donkey.

"I am old," wheezed the dog. "I can no longer go out hunting, and my master wants to do away with me, so I have left him. But now how am I going to earn a living?"

"Well," said the donkey, "I am on my way to Bremen to become a town musician. You may as well come with me. I can play the lute and you can beat the drum."

The dog agreed and the two set off together. It was not long before they met a cat with a face as sad as three rainy days.

"Well, now. What is the matter with you?" asked the donkey.

"I am old," mewed the cat forlornly. "I would rather sleep by the hearth than chase mice, and my mistress wants to drown me. So I have run away, but heaven knows what is to become of me."

"Come with us to Bremen," said the donkey, "and try your luck as a street musician. You can serenade while we play."

The cat thought this was a good idea, and the three continued their journey together. Soon they passed a yard where a cock was crowing with all his might.

"What in the world is the matter with you?" shouted the donkey.

"I overheard the mistress of the house tell the cook that I am to be Sunday supper's first course. This very evening, my neck is to be wrung," crowed the cock.

"You had better come with us," said the donkey. "We are going to Bremen to become town musicians, and your powerful voice is just what we need."

But Bremen was too far off to be reached in one day, and toward evening the animals came to some woods where they decided to spend the night. Just as they were settling down to rest, the cock spied a light burning in the distance, and he called to his friends that there must be a house not far off.

"Let us look for the house, for the woods are uncomfortable indeed," said the donkey, and so they all set off in the direction of the light, which grew brighter and brighter. At last the travelers found themselves at a house belonging to a band of robbers. The donkey peered into the window and saw a table set with a splendid feast, which the robbers were enjoying very much.

"Surely we poor creatures deserve that feast more than a den of thieves," said the donkey. And so he came up with a plan.

He placed his front hooves on the windowsill, the dog scrambled onto his back, the cat leapt onto the dog's back, and the cock perched on the cat's head. Then they struck up a tune. The donkey brayed, the dog barked, the cat mewed, the cock crowed, and they burst into the room, breaking the windowpane.

The robbers were all startled by the dreadful noise and, thinking that they were being attacked, they rushed out into the woods.

The four companions sat down at the table, and they ate and ate. When they had finished their meal they doused the fire and went to sleep.

Shortly after midnight, the robbers saw that no light was burning and that all was quiet. Their captain sent one of his men to investigate.

The man found everything quiet, but it was pitch-dark, so he went into the kitchen to strike a light. He mistook the glowing eyes of the cat for burning coals, and he held a match to them in order to kindle it. Now the cat didn't like this at all, so he flew at the unfortunate thief, spitting and scratching. The man cried out in terror and tried to run out the back door, but in the dark he stumbled over the dog, who bit him in the leg.

Yelling with pain, he ran across the courtyard, receiving a kick from the donkey as he passed. And the cock, who had been roused from his sleep by all the commotion, cried "Cock-a-doodle-doo!" as loudly as he could.

The poor robber ran back to his captain and said, "Sir, there is a dreadful witch in the house who scratched me with her long fingers. And at the door is a man with a knife who cut my leg. In the courtyard is a black monster who beat me with a huge club. But worst of all, on the roof sits a judge who called out 'Bring the rogue here!' So I fled for dear life."

After this the robbers never dared to go into the house again, but the Bremen Town musicians decided it was the perfect place for them and that they would remain in it forever. And for all we know, they may be living there still.

ABOUT THE ILLUSTRATOR

Daniel San Souci is a distinguished artist whose paintings have won numerous awards and honors. He is a graduate of the California College of Arts and Crafts, where he now teaches.

Mr. San Souci has illustrated many books, including *The Legend of Scarface*, which was named one of the ten best-illustrated children's books of 1978 by the New York Times.

Mr. San Souci lives and works in Oakland, California with his wife, Loretta, and his three children, Justin, Yvette, and Noelle.

DANIEL SAN SOUCI AND FRIENDS
A Self Portrait